DOGS SET VI

POINTERS

Nancy Furstinger
ABDO Publishing Company

visit us at
www.abdopub.com

Published by ABDO Publishing Company, 4940 Viking Drive, Edina, Minnesota 55435.
Copyright © 2006 by Abdo Consulting Group, Inc. International copyrights reserved in
all countries. No part of this book may be reproduced in any form without written
permission from the publisher. The Checkerboard Library™ is a trademark and logo of
ABDO Publishing Company.

Printed in the United States.

Cover Photo: Corbis
Interior Photos: Corbis pp. 5, 6, 7, 8, 9, 11, 13, 15, 17, 19, 21

Series Coordinator: Megan M. Gunderson
Editors: Megan M. Gunderson, Stephanie Hedlund
Art Direction: Neil Klinepier

Library of Congress Cataloging-in-Publication Data

Furstinger, Nancy.
    Pointers / Nancy Furstinger.
        p. cm. -- (Dogs. Set VI)
    Includes index.
    ISBN 1-59679-275-2
     1. Pointer (Dog breed)--Juvenile literature. I. Title.

SF429.P7F87 2005
636.752'5--dc22
                                                            2005040417

CONTENTS

THE DOG FAMILY

More than 12,000 years ago, people brought wolves into their homes. **Litters** of these pups grew up to be guards, hunters, and pets. These wolves were among the first animals tamed by humans. They developed into **domestic** dogs.

Today, almost 400 different **breeds** of dogs exist worldwide. Each has been bred for special purposes, including pointing out game and guiding the blind. They have become wonderful companions for people all over the world.

Dogs come in a variety of colors, shapes, and sizes. Despite their different appearances, all dogs belong to the same scientific **family**. It is called Canidae. This name comes from the Latin word *canis*, which means "dog."

Coyotes, foxes, jackals, and wolves are also members of the Canidae **family**. Dogs descended from wolves, and they share similar features. They both communicate through howling and growling. And, they have superior senses of smell and hearing.

Despite their differences in size and color, these dogs all belong to the Canidae family.

POINTERS

Pointers appeared in Spain, Portugal, eastern Europe, and the British Isles around the same time. They were first recorded in England around 1650. For this reason, they are sometimes called English pointers.

A pointer on point

Pointers are a mixture of the bloodhound, the greyhound, and foxhound **breeds**. At first, pointers were taken into the field and used to locate game. Then, greyhounds would come in to chase the prey.

Later, wing shooting with guns grew popular. This is when hunters shoot birds that are flying. They no longer needed a dog to chase the prey. So, the pointer became the favored gundog.

When a pointer spots game, it stiffens and points its nose toward the animal. This shows the hunter where the game is.

Sports people began bringing pointers into the United States in the early 1800s. In the late 1800s, pointers started becoming very popular there. In 1878, this popular **breed** was recognized by the **American Kennel Club (AKC)**.

What They're Like

Pointers are loyal and devoted, so they make wonderful family pets. They burst with energy. Pointers enjoy spending time both indoors and outdoors. However, they are not meant to live in cities. They need to be able to run!

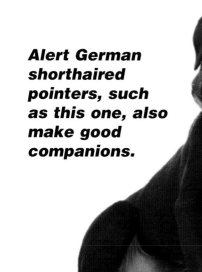

Alert German shorthaired pointers, such as this one, also make good companions.

In the field, pointers show endurance and courage. They quickly respond to sudden sounds and movements. These hunting dogs will range over a large

Pointers and other hunting dogs are trained to retrieve birds using a "gentle mouth" so they do not further harm the game.

area to search for the source of a sound. Pointers are eager to chase after wild birds.

Pointers are smart dogs that are eager to please. They learn quickly with positive obedience training. And pointers are perfect posers. So, they always stand out in dog shows and competitions.

COAT AND COLOR

The pointer has a short, compact coat. The fur is smooth with a sheen. Even after hunting, this **breed** usually just needs a quick brushing to get rid of burrs and debris.

The pointer's coat comes in four colors. These are black, liver, lemon, and orange. The coat can be either one solid color or a color combined with white. Most pointers have white coats with patches and markings of one of the four main colors.

The pointer's nose coloring depends on the shade of its fur. Darker-colored pointers have black or brown noses. Lighter-colored dogs may have paler noses.

This dog displays a typical pointer coloring, a white coat with patches of darker fur.

SIZE

The pointer is a muscular sporting dog. This **breed** combines power with spirited grace. Pointers have a strong body that is built for speed and energy. Their oval-shaped feet are well padded, with long, arched toes. The tail tapers to a point.

Pointers carry their head proudly. They have round, dark eyes. And, their nose sits high on the **muzzle**. Their nostrils are wide open to scent, or smell, the air for game. The breed's pointed ears hang close to the head.

Male pointers stand between 25 and 28 inches (64 and 71 cm) high at the shoulders. Females stand between 23 and 26 inches (58 and 66 cm) high. Males generally weigh 55 to 75 pounds (25 to 35 kg). And females weigh 45 to 65 pounds (20 to 30 kg).

A pointer's ears hang loose, even when the dog is alert or on point.

CARE

The pointer's coat is one of the thinnest of any **breed**. And it is sleek and shiny, so it is easy to groom. Once a week, use a rubber brush or a hound glove to remove loose hair. Then, rub the coat with a **chamois** to add gloss.

After brushing your pointer, make sure it is wearing a collar. Every dog should have a collar with an identification tag. This will let people know the name, address, and phone number to contact in case your best friend gets lost!

Besides you, your dog's next best friend is the veterinarian. During an annual checkup, your pointer will receive **vaccines** and a general health check. If you choose, your veterinarian can also **spay** or **neuter** your pet.

Every dog breed needs regular checkups and vaccines at the veterinarian, including this Weimaraner.

FEEDING

Your pointer will grow and gain energy by eating a healthy dog food. The food should have a protein listed as one of the first ingredients. Commercial dog food is available in canned, semimoist, and dry. The dry form can be good for your dog's teeth.

To prevent an upset stomach, bring home the same brand of food your pointer ate at the **breeder**'s. Later, you can slowly switch foods if you would like. The breeder can help recommend the right food for your growing dog.

Follow the feeding guide on the label. Match your dog's age and weight with the daily amount it should be fed. Two smaller meals per day are better for your adult pointer than one big meal. Many breeds like to be fed at the same time each day.

Make certain not to overfeed your pet. Keeping your dog lean will prevent a variety of health problems. Always offer fresh, clean water in a stainless steel bowl. And, treat your dog with healthy snacks such as dog biscuits.

If you give your dog a bone to chew on, make sure it is a safe size and made of a safe material, such as nylon.

THINGS THEY NEED

Pointers require daily exercise. These hunting dogs delight in long days in the field. They are **bred** to find and point game for hunters. With their speed and endurance, pointers can cover more ground than humans.

At home, this breed needs a fenced-in yard. Pointers can burn off excess energy in competitions. They stand out in obedience tests, hunting tests, and field trials.

Pointers quickly learn the house rules, especially if taught at a young age. In the house, a crate can offer them a safe and private place. This denlike bed is perfect for snoozing, traveling, and storing toys.

Pointers need lots of exercise and space to run. Playing with your dog will help you keep in shape, too!

PUPPIES

Mother pointers are **pregnant** for about 63 days. They give birth to an average of four to eight puppies in each **litter**. This is the average for medium-sized **breeds**.

Puppies spend most of their time sleeping, nursing, and growing. They can see and hear by two weeks of age. Then, they take their first steps. Pointers acquire the hunting instinct early. They can already hold point at a young age.

Puppies are **weaned** around seven weeks of age. They can be adopted after they are eight weeks old. **Purebred** pointers are available from qualified breeders. Or, visit a breed rescue or **Humane Society** to find puppies and older dogs to adopt.

20

Take your new pointer to a veterinarian to be **vaccinated** and checked for worms. Puppies get the first in a series of shots when they are between six and eight weeks old. A healthy pointer will live between 12 and 14 years.

Choosing a puppy is a difficult and important decision. Pay attention to both its personality and its health.

GLOSSARY

American Kennel Club (AKC) - an organization that studies and promotes interest in purebred dogs.

breed - a group of animals sharing the same appearance and characteristics. A breeder is a person who raises animals. Raising animals is often called breeding them.

chamois (SHA-mee) - a soft, bendable leather or cloth.

domestic - animals that are tame.

family - a group that scientists use to classify similar plants or animals. It ranks above a genus and below an order.

Humane Society - an organization that protects and cares for animals.

litter - all of the puppies born at one time to a mother dog.

muzzle - an animal's nose and jaws.

neuter (NOO-tuhr) - to remove a male animal's reproductive organs.

pregnant - having one or more babies growing within the body.

purebred - an animal whose parents are both from the same breed.

spay - to remove a female animal's reproductive organs.

vaccine (vak-SEEN) - a shot given to animals or humans to prevent them from getting an illness or disease.

wean - to accustom an animal to eat food other than its mother's milk.

WEB SITES

To learn more about pointers, visit ABDO Publishing Company on the World Wide Web at **www.abdopub.com**. Web sites about pointers are featured on our Book Links page. These links are routinely monitored and updated to provide the most current information available.

INDEX